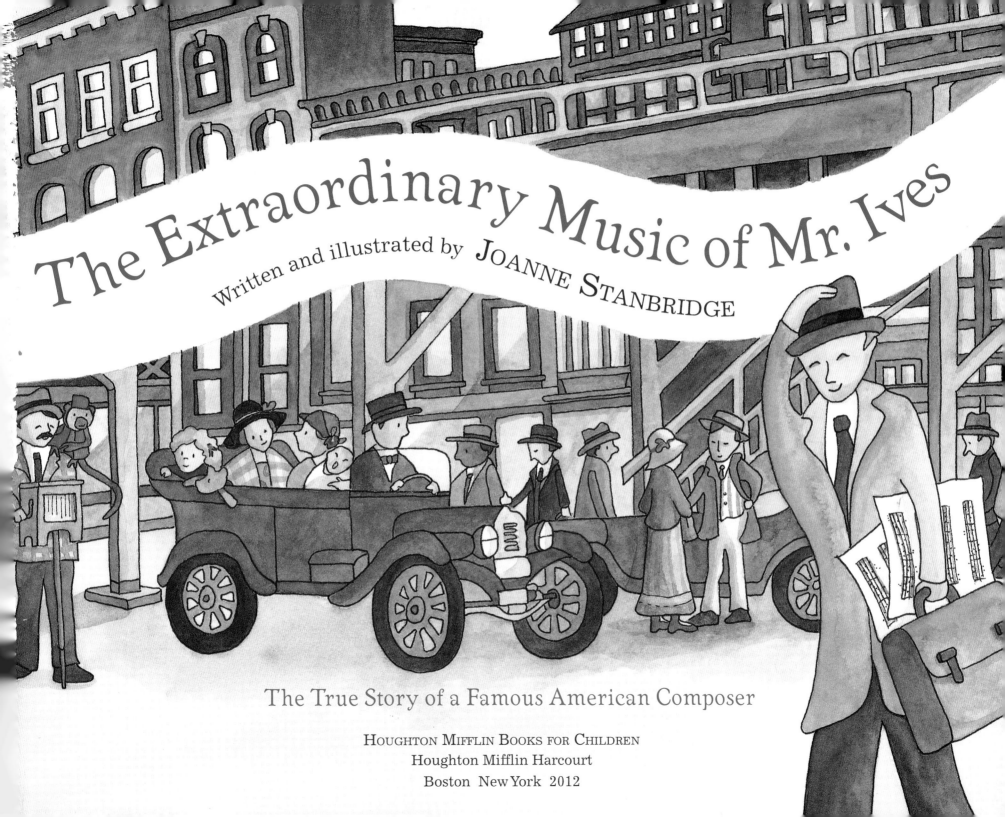

The Extraordinary Music of Mr. Ives

Written and illustrated by JOANNE STANBRIDGE

The True Story of a Famous American Composer

HOUGHTON MIFFLIN BOOKS FOR CHILDREN
Houghton Mifflin Harcourt
Boston New York 2012

One spring morning in New York City, a ship's whistle splits the air.

The ocean liner *Lusitania* is sailing from Pier 54. The whistle is so loud, it shakes the ground.

A few people cover their ears—but not Mr. Ives.

He grabs that big sound with both hands and shapes it into a song.

Even the most ordinary sounds are like songs to Mr. Ives.

He writes music that is as busy as a city street. There are train whistles in it, and football games and rowdy picnics and cars rushing past.

He hurries to his office, and even that ordinary place sounds like music to him. The *click click click* of adding machines and the murmur of *good morning* are so beautiful that he forgets to say *good morning* back.

All week long, Mr. Ives sits at his desk, adding and subtracting numbers.

Now and then he has to stop working and let his music come out. He lets it fly around the room, and when it lands, he writes it down.

People don't listen to his music. They don't like it. They don't understand it. They want familiar tunes and beautiful harmonies—not songs that are as bold as a city or as noisy as a traffic jam.

Mr. Ives writes his music down anyway. It lives inside him like a friend, and he carries it with him wherever he goes.

The year is 1915, and the nations of the world are at war. Everyone talks about guns and submarines. Everyone tries not to worry.

One day, terrible news comes. "The *Lusitania* is down!"

An enemy torpedo has struck the ocean liner. In just eighteen minutes, the great ship has gone down—down under the waves.

In the street, newsboys shout the headlines. The news spreads from office to office like fire. It hangs over the city like smoke, and it tastes of war.

When it reaches Mr. Ives, his music goes away. An awful loneliness seizes him, and his heart stretches out across the ocean—out into a dreadful silence.

Never before has an enemy blasted a ship full of innocent passengers.

How could it happen? What does it mean?

Mr. Ives can see questions in the faces of everyone who comes to the office.

Some talk softly. Others do their work in awful silence. All day, people struggle to understand.

Mr. Ives listens for the old familiar music of the office, but it has gone away. Even the city streets are hushed.

After work, he steps onto the platform to catch his train. Nearby, a hurdy-gurdy player is spinning a thin ribbon of song.

Mr. Ives knows that tune as well as he knows his own heartbeat. It was his father's favorite hymn.

> *In the sweet bye and bye*
> *we shall meet on that beautiful shore*

The faces of the people on the train platform are grim and sad, but the music is like a promise.

A worker with a shovel begins to sing. A banker stands beside him and hums.

One by one, others join in. They whistle or sing out the feelings that have been aching inside them all day. Soon, it seems as if the whole city is singing.

> *In the sweet bye and bye,*
> *we shall meet on that beautiful shore.*

Some voices creak. Others sing off-key. To Mr. Ives, the sound is as beautiful as raindrops falling together to make a river.

Up the song flows, into the evening sky, rolling out across the ocean to the sadness on the other side.

When the train comes, the passengers step inside quietly.

Their hearts are full of the strong old tune, and when it ends, they don't speak.

The train rattles uptown. A few voices hum or sing a few notes. Then they fall silent.

Mr. Ives carries that song with him, all the way home.

At his house in Connecticut he begins to write
the song down.

He mingles the old tune with street sounds.
The new song is

    a jumble of traffic noises
    a crash of danger
    the strains of the hurdy-gurdy, and then
    in the sweet bye and bye
    we shall meet on that beautiful shore

Mr. Ives names his new piece *From Hanover
Square North, at the End of a Tragic Day, the
Voice of the People Again Arose.*

But more than fifty years will pass before his song is performed. Like so much of Mr. Ives's music, it overflows with deep feelings and exciting new ideas, yet it is hard to play and hard to understand, so—year after year—it lies silent.

Meanwhile, Mr. Ives goes to his office. He adds and subtracts. He listens for music in the clatter of footsteps and the roar of engines.

Year after year, he scrawls down unexpected notes and rhythms until he, too, falls silent.

Thirteen years after Mr. Ives passes away, *From Hanover Square North* is performed for the first time.

It rockets around the concert hall and soars across the airwaves. Along with many of Mr. Ives's other long-silent pieces, it begins to find its way into the world.

At long last, more and more people begin to listen to Mr. Ives's music. More and more people begin to understand it.

Young composers are amazed by his big ideas. They grab those unusual sounds and make them their own.

Soon, echoes of Mr. Ives are heard in all kinds of music, from opera and ballet to orchestra concerts.

Pocahontas
Ballet – 1939
Music by Elliott Cook Carter, Jr.

Drums thud, feet stomp, and John Smith falls. One harsh chord gives way to a silence as wide as a sky. Even as a boy, this composer loved to experiment with sounds. Charles Ives urged him to study bold new forms of music at Harvard University.

The Tender Land
Opera – 1954
Music by Aaron Copland

With a thump and a holler, grandfather scolds the young farmhands. The music wraps itself around a noisy argument. Aaron Copland's big, rugged, "American" musical style was inspired by the music of Charles Ives.

On the Transmigration of Souls
Concert – 2002
Music by John Adams

The concert hall fills with the sound of rushing traffic, footsteps, and spoken words. When John Adams wrote music to commemorate the terrorist attacks of September 11, 2001, he was inspired by the music of Charles Ives, written nearly one hundred years earlier.

The man who wrote pieces that nobody would play is now known as one of the greatest American composers who ever lived.

When you hear music in everyday sounds—in the rumble of a motorcycle, the wail of a fire engine, or the busy chatter of a market—remember Mr. Ives.

After silence,
that which comes nearest
to expressing the
inexpressible
is music.

—Aldous Huxley

FOR THE HIGH-TEST GIRLS,
WITH LOVE AND GRATITUDE.

The author would like to thank the following for their expert help and guidance: the staff of the Irving S. Gilmore Music Library of Yale University, *Lusitania* researcher Michael Poirier, and the staff at the W. D. Jordan Music Library at Queen's University.

AUTHOR'S NOTE

Charles Ives heard music everywhere. He heard it in traffic noises and thunder, in the off-key enthusiasm of an amateur band and the heartfelt singing of untrained voices. He was one of the first composers to experiment seriously and methodically with these kinds of sounds, shaping them into a new kind of music.

His work overflowed with deep feelings and exciting new ideas, but it was hard to play and hard to understand. Musicians laughed at it or grew angry; nobody would perform it. Ives made his living selling insurance, but he spent every spare moment composing music.

In May 1915, he was at his office in Manhattan when news arrived that a German torpedo had sunk the passenger ship *Lusitania*, which was sailing from New York City to England. More than one thousand died. Among the survivors were six-year-old Helen Smith and a Canadian journalist named Ernest Cowper, who helped her to escape.

Charles Ives watched his fellow commuters respond to the tragedy by bursting into song. He was deeply moved, and he shaped the experience into a musical piece that became the final movement of his Second Orchestral Set. The piece was finished in the autumn of 1915, and its first performance was given by the Chicago Symphony Orchestra in February 1967, thirteen years after Ives's death. The biographer David Wooldridge called it his "most exalted work."

Ives was ahead of his time. Many of the qualities that would make twentieth-century music so unique were heard first in his work.

FURTHER READING AND LISTENING

Ghost Liners: Exploring the World's Greatest Lost Ships by Robert D. Ballard, Rick Archbold, and Ken Marschall (Boston: Little, Brown, 1998).

What Charlie Heard: The Story of the American Composer Charles Ives by Mordicai Gerstein (New York: Farrar, Straus and Giroux, 2001).

Listen to "In the Sweet Bye-and-Bye" on the Internet archive website www.archive.org/details/TheLewisFamily-InTheSweetByAndBy.

Oral History of American Music: Charles Ives is a free netcast from the Yale School of Music. Family, friends, and colleagues share their memories of the composer: music.yale.edu/news/?p=2279.

SELECTED SOURCES

The descriptions of Ives's experiences on May 7, 1915, are based on his own words as recorded in the book *Memos*, edited by John Kirkpatrick (New York: W. W. Norton, 1972).

Adams, John. *On the Transmigration of Souls*. New York Philharmonic conducted by Lorin Maazel. Nonesuch 79816-2.

Ballard, Robert D., and Spencer Dunmore. *Exploring the Lusitania*. New York: Warner Books, 1995.

Burkholder, J. Peter. *Charles Ives and His World*. Princeton, N.J.: Princeton University Press, 1996.

Charles Ives, *Orchestral Set No. 2*. Chicago Symphony Orchestra conducted by Morton Gould. RCA Victor LM 2959, 1967.

Charles Ives Society, www.charlesives.org.

Cowell, Henry, and Sidney Robertson Cowell. *Charles Ives and His Music*. New York: Oxford University Press, 1955.

Kalafus, Jim, and Michael Poirier. "Lest We Forget," *Lusitania* resource on the *Encyclopedia Titanica* website at www.encyclopedia-titanica.org/Lusitania-lest-we-forget.html.

Perlis, Vivian. *Charles Ives Remembered: An Oral History*. New Haven: Yale University Press, 1974.

Simpson, Colin. *The Lusitania*. Boston: Little, Brown, 1973.

Swafford, Jan. *Charles Ives: A Life with Music*. New York: W. W. Norton, 1998.

Copyright © 2012 by Joanne Stanbridge

Houghton Mifflin Books for Children is an imprint of Houghton Mifflin Harcourt Publishing Company.

www.hmhbooks.com

The text of this book is set in Excelsior and Artcraft. The illustrations are ink and watercolor on cold-press Arches watercolor paper.

Aldous Huxley, "The Rest Is Silence," *Music at Night: and Other Essays*. London: Chatto and Windus, 1931.

Photo of Charles Ives at left by Bill Joli, MSS 14-128, Charles Ives Papers, Irving S. Gilmore Music Library, Yale University.

LCCN 2011048033
ISBN 978-0-547-23866-1

Manufactured in China
SCP 10 9 8 7 6 5 4 3 2 1
4500361369